ETHICAL HACKING

ETHICAL HACKING

*The Complete Beginners Guide to
Basic Security and Penetration Testing*

Marc Stanford

ETHICAL HACKING

Copyright© 2019 by Aculeatus Limited
All Rights Reserved

MARC STANFORD
amazon.com/author/marcstanford

Printed in the United States of America
First Printing: October 2019
ISBN-13: 9781698148427

Imprint: Independently published
Cover designed by pro_ebookcovers, FL, USA

No parts of this book may be reproduced, duplicated or transmitted in any form or by any means, electronic or mechanical, including photocopies, recordings or any support without the written permission of the author or publisher. The only exception is by a reviewer, who may quote short excerpts in a review.

All the methods shown in the book are for educational purposes only. The author assumes no responsibility for improper use of the techniques shown. Under no circumstances will any blame or legal responsibility be held against the publisher, or author, for any damages, reparation, or monetary loss due to the information contained within this book. Either directly or indirectly.

This copyright protected book is for personal use only. To amend, sell, distribute, use or quote any part, or the content within this book, without the consent of the author or publisher, is not permitted.

To all clueless victims of cyberattacks

CONTENTS

INTRODUCTION TO ETHICAL HACKING	1
THE LABORATORY	3
KALI LINUX COMMANDS	8
NETWORK THEORY	14
CORPORATE NETWORKS	19
INFORMATION GATHERING	22
NETWORK SCANNING	28
BANNER GRABBING	33
ENUMERATION	35
CONCLUSION	37
ABOUT THE AUTHOR	38

All warfare is based on deception
- Sun Tzu

INTRODUCTION TO ETHICAL HACKING

The purpose of this book is to reveal an easy way to learn how to become a good ethical hacker. One does not need special skills, or many years of programming experience to become an ethical hacker. Ethical hacking and ethical hacker are terms used to describe hacking performed by a company or an individual to help identify potential threats on a computer or network. An ethical hacker attempts to bypass system security and search for any weak points that could be exploited by malicious hackers. Ethical hacking cannot be considered as a cybercrime unless the hacker disobeys the rules, and does not follow the code of the universal ethics agreement. Ethical Hacking is good, or you can say, White Hat Hackers are ethical as they don't use their skills for illegal purposes. They use their IT-skills for protecting people from the Black Hat Hackers and usually as computer or cybersecurity experts. The purpose of ethical hacking is to evaluate the level of cybersecurity and to identify vulnerabilities in systems, networks, or system infrastructure. It includes finding and attempting to exploit any weak points to determine whether unauthorized access or other malicious activities are possible.

The term ethical hacker has received criticism at times from people who say that there is no such thing as an ethical hacker. Hacking is hacking, no matter how you look at it, and those who do the hacking are commonly referred to as computer criminals or cybercriminals. However, the work that ethical hackers do for organizations has helped improve system security and turned out to be quite productive and successful.

For hacking to be deemed ethical, a hacker must obey these four rules:
1. Express permission to probe the network and attempt to identify potential security risks.
2. Respect the individual's or company's privacy.
3. Close out your work, not leaving anything open for you or someone else to exploit at a later time.
4. Inform the software developer or hardware manufacturer about any security vulnerabilities you locate in their software or hardware, if not already known by the company.

As the complexity of security vulnerabilities has grown, so too has the need for ethical hackers and their prominence in businesses across the globe. Taking a proactive approach to security can help organizations better protect their data and reputations, as well as save money. The elevated threat landscape, therefore, urgently dictates the need for a comprehensive, real-world assessment of an organization's security posture. This assessment is the first vital step to enact effective security policies, procedures, and infrastructure that prevents or mitigates the effects of a data breach.

To be a successful ethical hacker, you must know how to scan, test, hack, and secure systems. You need a thorough understanding of how intruders escalate privileges and how to secure a system. Ethical hackers need hands-on experience and can conduct robust vulnerability assessments. They're familiar with Intrusion Detection, Policy Creation, Social Engineering, DDoS Attacks, Buffer Overflows, and Virus Creation.

Ethical hackers use their skills and many of the same methods and techniques to test and bypass organizations' IT security as their unethical counterparts, who are referred to as black hat hackers. However, rather than taking advantage of any vulnerabilities they find for personal gain, ethical hackers document them and provide advice about how to remediate them so organizations can strengthen their overall security. Ethical hackers generally find security exposures in insecure system configurations, known and unknown hardware or software vulnerabilities, as well as operational weaknesses in process or technical countermeasures. Any organization that has a network connected to the Internet or provides an online service should consider subjecting it to penetration testing conducted by ethical hackers. The following chapters describe the necessary knowledge and content of laboratories, Linux commands, mind maps, network theory, enterprise networks, information gathering, network scanning, banner grabbing, inference, vulnerability assessment, exploitation, and post-exploitation.

THE LABORATORY

The first task on the way to become an ethical hacker is to build your laboratory. Use this setup guide to prepare your lab environment for various hacking methods and developing penetration strategies.

Your **computer** can be a laptop or desktop. It should meet the following minimum requirements:
   Intel Core i5 3.2 GHz 64-bit CPU or better (multiple cores is preferred)
   16 GB RAM (32 GB or more is recommended)
   200 GB free disk space, 7200 RPM or faster drive (SSD is preferred)
   DVD drive
   1 Ethernet network adapter
   17" LC monitor
   Mouse, sound card
   Internet access, Wireless network adapter (built-in or USB)

The following **operating systems** are needed in the laboratory:
   Kali 2018.3 VM 64 Bit 7z
   https://images.offensive-security.com/virtual-images/kali-linux-2018.3-vm-amd64.7z
   Windows Server 2016 ISO (licensed or evaluation)
   https://www.microsoft.com/en-us/evalcenter/evaluate-windows-server-2016

   Windows Server 2012 R2 ISO (licensed or evaluation)
   https://www.microsoft.com/en-us/evalcenter/evaluate-windows-server-2012-r2
   Windows 8.1 64-bit ISO - be SURE to select 64-bit!
   https://www.microsoft.com/en-us/software-download/windows8ISO
   Ubuntu 16.04.3 Desktop 64bit ISO
   http://old-releases.ubuntu.com/releases/16.04.3/ubuntu-16.04.3-desktop-amd64.iso

Metasploitable 2
https://sourceforge.net/projects/metasploitable/files/Metasploitable2

You require these necessary **support-software packages**:
VMWare Workstation 15 Player for Windows (alternatively, VMWare Workstation Pro or Oracle Virtual Box)
https://www.vmware.com/products/workstation-player/workstation-playerevaluation.html
7zip for 64-bit Windows
https://www.7-zip.org/a/7z1805-x64.exe
Opera Browser for Windows
https://www.opera.com/computer/thanks?ni=stable&os=windows
A PDF reader such as Adobe Acrobat Reader or Foxit PDF Reader
https://www.foxitsoftware.com/downloads/#Foxit-Reader/
Mozilla Thunderbird for Windows
https://www.thunderbird.net/en-US/
Mail Enable Standard Edition (Free) Email Server
http://www.mailenable.com/standard_edition.asp

Also required are several **hacking-tools:**
These tools need to be downloaded and organized on your host machine. Please drag and drop these tools as needed to your Windows guests during the activities.

- On your host computer, create the folder C:\Hacking Tools.
- In your antivirus program, make a permanent exemption for C:\Hacking Tools.
- While downloading and organizing the tools, temporarily shut off your antivirus program.
- Inside of C:\Hacking Tools, create the following subfolders to organize your downloaded hacking tools.

Some modules either do not have activities or do not need additional software; therefore, they don't need folders.
C:\HackingTools\
Module 2-Footprinting Reconnaissance
Module 3-Network Scanning
Module 4-Enumeration
Module 5-Vulnerability Analysis
Module 6-Malware Threats

Module 7-Sniffing
Module 9-Denial of Service
Module 11-Hacking Web Servers
Module 15-System Hacking
Module 17-Evading IDS Firewalls Honeypots

Download and place each of the following tools in their respective folders. Make sure your antivirus (real-time protection) is shut off.

Please bear in mind that, Chrome and Internet Explorer browsers may still refuse to download some of the tools, especially the denial-of-service applications. Consider using Opera instead.

The following **additional hardware** is necessary for some of the activities. If you don't have this hardware, you can watch the respective activity videos without performing the tasks yourself.

Older Android phone, version 4.4 (KitKat) to 6.0.1 (Marshmallow). The phone does NOT need a SIM card or cellular plan. It just needs to be WiFi capable.

WiFi capable mobile device such as a phone, tablet, or laptop. The Android phone (above) can also be used.

WiFi router such as a Linksys WRT54-G or similar. Must support both WEP and WPA.

External Wi-Fi network adapter such as an Alfa AWUS036NHA Wireless B/G/N USB or similar.

The device must be capable of running the Aircrack-ng suite in promiscuous mode on Kali Linux.

USB thumb drive, formatted with the FAT32 file system, with at least 50 KB of free space.

❖ Preparing the Host Machine

You can install some software such as VMware Workstation 15 Professional or Oracle Virtual Box and Opera, PDF Reader, and 7zip.

You can set the Virtual Box or VMware Workstation environment.

Create Windows Server 2016 VM

Recommendation: If possible, create all virtual machines on the
C: drive. Creating them on an external hard drive can result in poor performance.

❖ Installation of the operating system

You can install "Windows_Server_2016_Datacenter_EVAL_enus_ 14393_ refresh.ISO" with Virtual Machine Wizard and then check the ID subnet and set it. Install Chrome browser and MailEnable Email Server and set up Mailboxes, configure SNMP.

There are several ways to construct the laboratory; therefore, you can build the laboratory environment according to your requirements. You can build a Linux virtual laboratory with VirtualBox more easily. Kali Linux is one of the most widely used operating systems for penetration testing, and it should be in your arsenal. Visit the Kali website and download the ISO file. After the file is downloaded, continue and create a new virtual machine with Kali Linux. To create a new virtual machine, please open up VirtualBox.

- After you open up the program, you need to click the "New" button. A window pops up, and you need to enter the name of the operating system, the type of operating system, and the version. For Kali, the name of the operating system is "Kali Linux," the type of operating system is "Linux," and the version is "Debian (64-bit)". Then click the "next" button.
- The author recommends a minimum of 2GB disc space for Kali Linux. Other operating systems vary, but reserving 2GB or more to every operating system is on the safe side. Use the slider and drag it to 2048 MB and click the "Next" button.
- Next, you need to specify whether or not you want to create a virtual hard disk. In this book, we choose the option "Create a virtual hard disk now."
- Then click the "Create" button. The recommended size is 8GB, but you are going to use 20GB, which is set in a minute. If the free space on your hard drive is limited, then you may want to stick with 8 GB.
- Afterward, you need to choose the hard disk file type. You can keep the default set to "VDI (VirtualBox Disk Image)" and click "Next."
- Now you need to choose if you want the hard drive dynamically allocated or set to a fixed size. You can select "Fixed Size" and click "Next."
- And finally, you need to set the virtual hard disk size by adjusting the slider to 20.00 GB. You can leave the name as default "Kali Linux" and click the "Create" button.

Now that you have your virtual machine created and configured, you need to install the operating system. If you have installed Kali Linux before then, this procedure won't be new to you.

- To start, you need to make sure that your Kali Linux virtual machine is selected and then click the "Start" button in VirtualBox.
- When you click the "Start" button, a window pops up where you select the start-up disk. At this point Kali Linux ISO file comes in handy that you downloaded earlier. Click the folder button and navigate to the ISO file and select it.
- When it is selected, click the "Start" button. A new window now opens up, and you start going through the process of installing Kali Linux. At the Boot Menu, select "Graphical Install" and press "Enter."

The system guides you through the installation options. If you have never installed Kali Linux before, then the author recommends watching a video (https://www.youtube.com/watch?v=f5NUcEd1EYA) on how to build a hacking lab with VirtualBox. This video is a step-by-step guide through the installation procedure.

Furthermore, if you plan on using a WiFi adapter in the future to sniff and capture packets, then you should also learn how to connect ALFA AWUS036H to Kali Linux in VirtualBox.

KALI LINUX COMMANDS

Kali Linux is the most famous Pen Testing Linux Distro, which is for now based on Debian, developed by Offensive Security. Kali Linux is also used to hack WiFi passwords. Hackers and security researchers commonly use Kali Linux Hacking Commands.

The most frequently used Kali Linux hacking commands are:
- CD

Cd: to change the active directory, this command is used. By default, when you start your system and launch the terminal app, you are at home directory of the given *username/login*. Look below for a few useful commands to change the directory.

Cd.. let's assume you are in directory */root/fruits/apple*. If you type *cd..* in the command terminal, you end up in */root/fruits*. If you give the same command again, you end up in */root/*.

Cd / this will make a new directory for you. For example, if you type *cd movies*, it creates a new current directory name as movies as a working directory.
- PWD

Pwd: typing this command in the terminal shows the working folder you are in, or it shows the active directory. In other words, it prints the working or active folder or directory for you.
- LS/LA

ls: this command helps the user to view all files or directories in a given folder or working directory. No matter the working directory contains what type of files, this command prints them all on the terminal screen.

-ls – la: again, executing this command enlists all folders and files in a given or working directory. It even shows you the hidden folders in a directory. You can create a folder or file wherever you want using the above command.
- MKDIR

Mkdir: to make a new folder or directory, you can use this command. All you need to do is to type *mkdir space directory name*, and there you have the new directory.

For example, if you would like to create a directory with the name of myMovies, you type *mkdir myMovies* and create a folder named myMovies in the current working directory. To see if the directory was successfully created or not type *ls*.

To access the newly created folder type *cd myMovies,* and it takes you into the newly created folder or directory.

- CP

Cp: this command is used to copy any file or folder. For example, if you wish to copy a file abc.mp4 to folder myMovies then type the command *Cp abc.mp4 /myMovies*

- MV

Mv: this command is used to move a file from one location to the other. The command structure is very much similar to the above cp command. Again, using the same example to move the file named as abc.mp4 to folder myMovies, the syntax of the command is: *mv abc.mp4 /myMovies*.

- RM

Rm: this command is used to remove any file.

To remove a file, all you need is to type *rm abc.mp4*. To remove a directory or a folder, type this command and press enter: *rm –rf foldername/directoryName*.

Important: **Never** use this command *rf /* in combination with rm as it removes everything from the given computer.

- Nano

Nano: to read a file using command terminal nano commands are pretty useful. For example, if you would like to read a file named log.txt, here is the syntax for this: *nano log.txt*. This command opens the text file if it exists.

To close the file after viewing it, press the keys *ctrl+x*. If you would like to close it using the command terminal, look at the bottom of the opened file; there are some other uses full short keys and commands. For example, to justify the text, you can use the ^j, and to cut text, you can use ^k.

Other commands are related to writing out, where is, replace, and get help. Note these commands are for a text file. A complete list of Kali Linux commands can be found in the public domain.

MIND MAPS

Mind Maps are a visual and graphical way to organize your thoughts and to represent ideas and concepts around one topic using words, colors, images and numbers to highlight ideas and draw connections. Using mind mapping enables you to learn faster, communicate more efficiently, and brainstorm more effectively. Whether you're planning a project at work or writing a scientific paper, mind mapping can help you save tremendous amounts of time. During your work as an ethical hacker, and a penetration tester, you collect a great deal of information that needs to be organized efficiently.

Invented by **Tony Buzan** in the 1960s, mind mapping is much more than drawing: It's a framework to help you thoroughly think through ideas, and show how topics and ideas are connected and allowing with more flexibility than an outline or list affords. You might say that Mind Maps are thinking tools that help to structure information and helping users to better analyze, comprehend, synthesize, recall, and generate new ideas. Just as in every great idea, its power lies in its simplicity.

Mind mapping can be a solo or team activity, and they can be used for all types of tasks: learning, thinking through ideas, strategic planning, mapping out processes, or organizing overwhelming amounts of information. In a mind map, as opposed to traditional note-taking or a linear text, information is structured in a way that resembles much more closely how your brain works. Since it is an activity that is both analytical and artistic, it engages your brain in a much, much more productive way, helping in all its cognitive functions. Mind mapping avoids dull, linear thinking, jogging your creativity, and making note-taking fun again.

Mind Maps are of two types: maps where the benefit is mainly in the **process** of making the map, the thinking process, the memory jogging, the stimulation of new ideas and associations, and maps where the benefit is the map as a reference and communication point. Notably, both association and imagination can be used when creating mind maps and improving memory processes. By including words, images, colors, and branches, the mind map helps the map-maker to place information into memory.

Drawing a mind map is quite simple: Start in the middle of a blank page (landscape orientation recommended), writing or drawing the idea you intend to develop. Develop the related subtopics around this central topic, connecting each of them to the center with a line. Repeat the same process for the subtopics, generating lower-level subtopics as you see fit, connecting each of those to the corresponding subtopic.

Some more recommendations: Use colors, drawings, and symbols copiously. Be as visual as you can, and your brain will thank you. Keep the topics labels as short as possible, keeping them to a single word – or, better yet, to only a picture. Especially in your first mind maps, the temptation to write a complete phrase is enormous, but always look for opportunities to shorten it to a single word or figure – your mind map will be much more effective that way. Vary text size, color, and alignment. Vary the thickness and length of the lines. Provide as many visual cues as you can to emphasize important points. Every little bit helps to engage your brain.

Recommendations for foundation structures used for mind mapping are:
- Start in the center with an image of the topic, using at least three colors.
- Use images, symbols, codes, and dimensions throughout your Mind Map.
- Select key words and print using upper- or lower-case letters.
- Each word or image must be alone and sitting on its own line.
- The lines must be connected, starting from the central image.
- The central lines are thicker, organic, and flowing, becoming thinner as they radiate out from the center.
- Make the lines the same length as the word/image.
- Develop your style of Mind Mapping.
- Use emphasis and show associations in your Mind Map.
- Keep the Mind Map clear by using radial hierarchy, numerical order, or outlines to embrace your branches.

Why is it recommended for ethical hackers to use Mind Maps instead of lists or outlines? Because lists always get long, and they assign importance in terms of where the item is on the list. If something is further down, it's inherently less critical. If you have topics that are on a similar level, it's hard to show that in a list. Mind maps are easy to reorganize if you decide something belongs to something else. In other words, instead of capturing information linearly by default, mind maps can show–and help you discover–connections between different topics, the way your mind works.

The author hopes that as a designated ethical hacker, you are convinced and ready to use Mind Maps for organizing information. If yes, then it's time to select the right Mind Mapping software.

Each of the best mind mapping tools comes with unique benefits, but they all offer at least the following:

- **Unlimited canvas:** If your mind mapping canvas has size limitations, it can cut your creativity short just because you run out of the canvas space. Even if you can't see your entire mind map at once, an unlimited canvas allows you to brainstorm until you are done.
- **Ability to attach files:** Sometimes using text only is not enough to convey your ideas, or you want to include an external file as part of your brainstorming. In all of the best mind mapping apps, you can attach links, images, and other files to your mind map.
- **Collaboration features:** Any mind map apps that are built on the cloud should make it easy for multiple users to collaborate and comment on the canvas.
- All of the best desktop apps allow adequate cloud file sharing/syncing across devices so that multiple users can access and revise the mind map.
- **Ability to save and export:** These apps all allow you to save your map and re-edit it at a future date, and they all offer the ability to either share maps online or export them.

The best 10 Mind Mapping Tools of 2019 (in alphabetical order) are:

Mindly (macOS, iOS, Android) for mobile mind mapping;
https://www.mindlyapp.com/
Draw.io (Web, macOS, Linux, Windows, Chrome OS) for free
mind mapping
https://about.draw.io/
iMindMap (macOS, Windows, iOS) for performing an in-depth analysis
https://www.ayoa.com/imindmap/software/
MindMup (Web) for creating public mind maps
https://www.mindmup.com/
MindMeister (Web, iOS, Android, macOS, Windows) for team collaboration
https://www.mindmeister.com/

Scapple (macOS, Windows) for fluid, non-traditional mind mapping
https://www.literatureandlatte.com/scapple/overview
SmartDraw (Web) for linear mind mapping
https://www.smartdraw.com/
Stormboard (Web) for in-person mind mapping sessions
https://stormboard.com/
SimpleMind (macOS, Windows, iOS, Android) for creating mind maps from PDFs
https://simplemind.eu/
LucidChart (Web, iOS, Android) for turning mind maps into an organized flowchart
https://www.lucidchart.com/pages/

NETWORK THEORY

This chapter aims to present you with an overview of the primary services and network protocols. A protocol is a particular set of rules for having a conversation between two computers to convey a specific set of information. A standard - and in the networking arena, many protocols are standards - is a document that specifies something that has the overwhelming support and agreement of the standards-making body. A protocol is a standard set of rules that allow electronic devices to communicate with each other. Protocols exist for several different applications. Examples include wired networking, e.g., Ethernet, wireless networking, e.g., 802.11ac, and Internet communication, e.g., IP.

The Internet and most other data networks work by organizing data into small pieces called packets. Because protocols like Internet Protocol often work together in layers, some data embedded inside a packet formatted for one protocol can be in the format of some other related protocol; a method called encapsulation.

A well-defined protocol helps different systems to communicate and to exchange information. There are several broad types of networking protocols, including Network communication protocols: Basic data communication protocols, such as TCP/IP and HTTP. Network security protocols: Implement security over network communications and include HTTPS, SSL, and SFTP. Generally speaking, networks have three types of protocols: communication protocols, such as Ethernet; management protocols, such as the Simple Mail Transfer Protocol (SMTP); and security protocols, such as Secure Shell (SSH).

In telephony, a functional protocol is a type of protocol that is used to carry signaling messages between endpoints. Such a protocol is used to control the operation of devices at each end of the link. The adjective functional is used to describe protocols that are aware of the system state of the endpoints.

The standard network protocols are:
    TCP/IP (Transmission Control Protocol/Internet Protocol) suite.

ARP (Address Resolution Protocol)
DHCP (Dynamic Host Configuration Protocol)
DNS (Domain Name System)
FTP (File Transfer Protocol)
HTTP (HyperText Transfer Protocol)
HTTPS (HyperText Transfer Protocol Secure)

Network protocols made the modernization of the Internet possible. Such protocols allow computers to communicate with other computers without users having to know what is happening in the background.

The critical elements of a protocol are syntax, semantics, and timing.
- Syntax. The term syntax refers to the structure or format of the data, meaning the order in which they are presented.
- Semantics. The word semantics refers to the meaning of each section of bits.
- Timing. The term timing refers to two characteristics.

Not all protocols are standards; some are proprietary. Not all standards are protocols; some govern other layers than communication. A protocol is not a set of rules. This is why programs implement a protocol and comply with a standard. The difference between service and protocol is that service is a function that is provided by one program or machine for another while the protocol is a set of formal rules describing how to transmit or exchange data, especially across a network.

In computer networking, a network service is an application running at the network application layer and above that provides data storage, manipulation, presentation, communication, or other capabilities, which is often implemented using a client-server or peer-to-peer architecture based on application layer network protocols. Each service is usually provided by a server component running on one or more computers (often a dedicated server computer offering multiple services) and accessed via a network by client components running on other devices. However, the client and server components can both be run on the same machine. Clients and servers will often have a user interface, and sometimes other hardware associated with it. Examples are:
- The Domain Name System (DNS) translates domain names to Internet protocol (IP) addresses and the Dynamic Host Configuration Protocol (DHCP) to assign networking configuration information to network hosts.

- Authentication servers identify and authenticate users, provide user account profiles, and may log usage statistics.
- E-mail, printing, and distributed (network) file system services are essential services on local area networks. They require users to have permission to access the shared resources.

A service network is a structure that brings together several entities to deliver a particular service. A service network can also be defined as a collection of people and information brought together on the internet to provide a specific service or achieve a common business objective. Each service is usually provided by a server component running on one or more computers (often a dedicated server computer offering multiple services) and accessed via a network by client components running on other devices. The client and server components can both run on the same machine.

A host is a computer, connected to other computers for which it provides data or services over a network. In theory, every computer connected to a network acts as a host to other peers on the network. In essence, a host reflects the logical relationship of two or more computers on a network.

> Internet - Service Protocols

Service protocols deal with identifying which service is needed to display the contents of each packet. HTTP (HyperText Transfer Protocol) is the service protocol that allows users to receive information from the World Wide Web. The following table shows a list of commonly used Service Protocols.

Topic	List
TCP- and UDP-based protocols	List of TCP and UDP port numbers
Automation	List of automation protocols
Bluetooth	List of Bluetooth protocols
Electronic trading	List of electronic trading protocols
File transfer	Comparison of file transfer protocols
Instant messaging	Comparison of instant messaging protocols
Internet Protocol	List of IP protocol numbers
Link aggregation	List of Nortel protocols
OSI protocols	List of network protocols (OSI model)
Protocol stacks	List of network protocol stacks
Routing	List of ad hoc routing protocols
Routing	List of routing protocols
Web services	List of web service protocols

> Hacking in Networks

In computer networking, hacking is any technical effort to manipulate the normal behavior of network connections and connected systems. Today, however, hacking and hackers are most commonly associated with malicious programming attacks on networks and computers over the Internet. Network hacking is an offensive branch of computer security related to network hacking and the penetration of a target via the networking services or equipment.

Examples of network hacking tools include
- Kismet: Wireless Network Hacking, Sniffing & Monitoring
- THC-Hydra: The fast and flexible Network Login Hacking Tool
- Infernal Twin 2.6.11: Automated Wireless Hacking Suite
- Firesheep: Social network Session Stealing/Hijacking Tool

Network hacking would also include WLAN hacking, WiFi hacking, wireless hacking, and Cisco hacking, which would rely on various types of network hacking software. Nowadays, the majority of all hacking takes place across some network, be it a private network or LAN, the public Internet, a darknet, public radio networks, or any other kind. Currently, the best resources and networking hacking tools are:

> RandIP: Network Mapper to find Servers
RandIP is a nim-based network mapper application that generates random IP addresses and uses sockets to test whether the connection is valid or not with additional tests for Telnet and SSH. RandIP – Network Mapper Features HTTP and HTTPS enumeration Python enumeration exploits SSH enumeration exploits Logger and error-code handler SSH and Telnet Timeouts

> Enumall: Subdomain Discovery using Recon-ng & AltDNS
Enumall is a Python-based tool that helps you do subdomain discovery using only one command by combining the abilities of Recon-ng and AltDNS. This gives you the ability to run multiple domains within the same session. The tool only has one module that needs an API key (/api/google_site)

> Sublist3r: Fast Python Subdomain Enumeration Tool

Sublist3r is a Python-based tool designed to enumerate subdomains of websites using OSINT. It helps penetration testers and bug hunters collect and gather subdomains for the domain they are targeting. It also integrates with *subbrute* for subdomain brute-forcing with word lists. Features of Sublist3r Subdomain Enumeration Tool It enumerates subdomains using many search engines.

➤ RDPY: RDP Security Tool for hacking Remote Desktop Protocol
RDPY is an RDP Security Tool in Twisted Python with RDP Man in the Middle proxy support, which can record sessions and Honeypot functionality. RDPY is a pure Python implementation of the Microsoft RDP (Remote Desktop Protocol) protocol (client- and server-side). RDPY is built over the event-driven network engine Twisted. RDPY support standard.

➤ SNIFFlab: Create your own MITM Test Environment
SNIFFlab is a set of scripts in Python that enable you to create your MITM test environment for packet sniffing through a WiFi access point. Mostly, itis a WiFi hotspot that is continually collecting all the packets transmitted across it. All connected clients' HTTPS communications are subjected to a "Man-in-the-middle" attack.

CORPORATE NETWORKS

A network is a set of hardware devices connected, either physically or logically, to allow them to exchange information. A corporate network is a group of computers connected in a building or in a particular area, which is all owned by the same company or institutions. Having a good understanding of most network devices and their functions helps you carry out a penetration test in a much more accurate and effective way.

Network management includes the exploitation, incorporation, and coordination of the hardware, software, and human fundamentals to monitor, test, poll, configure, analyses, evaluate, and control the network and element resources to meet the real-time, operational, performance, and quality of service requirements at a reasonable cost. Corporate Network Management (CNM) provides network and communication services to the entire organization.

The whole idea of the corporate network formation is that everyone should be working together as one unit. That should be the aim of the corporate network. People may be occupied in different buildings, departments, and organizational structures around the world. But a corporate network needs to bring them all together, help them communicate and share resources, and protect and advance the interests of the corporate entity.

A synonym for the corporate network is the term enterprise network, which is defined as an enterprise's communications backbone that helps connect computers and related devices across departments and workgroup networks, facilitating insight and data accessibility. A corporate network is about keeping both machines and people connected.

Network management is the main factor for corporate business in the competitive world. Network management can be categorized into
- Network provisioning- Network Planning, Network Design, Responsibility of the engineering group

- Network maintenance- Network Installations, Network Repairs Facilities Installations, and Maintenance
- Network operations- Fault Management, Configuration Management, Accounting Management, Performance Management, Security Management

CNM support programs help to improve network performance and response, provide efficient, reliable system backup and ensure secure network protection, reduces systems management cost, and creates dependable wired and wireless access to business information and resources.

- Wireless Network Security

Corporate networks are protected by many layers of security, one of which is physical security. It probably includes going through multiple layers of physical security controls, such as parking access gates, fences, and security guards. Employees can easily get access to the facility, but getting access to the data center is usually limited to a select group of individuals.

Wireless networking cannot rely on physical security to completely secure it. Yes, it is possible to use directional antennas to contain the signal inside your four walls or even use specially designed mesh surfaces inside your walls to create a Faraday cage for WiFi signals, but that is neither foolproof nor 100% secure.

Worse, those techniques generally don't work with all wireless technologies, and it won't protect your network against a hot-shot user who puts a generic AP in his office so that he can work on his laptop from the conference room.

- Backup Tapes

Backup tapes are created in nearly every corporate network. How much data is regularly secured on backup tapes depends both on the corporation's data retention policies and whether they are being followed?

Tape backups are frequently stored off-site, and older tapes may even be stored without an adequate tape inventory or labeling, so it may require significant time and expense to assess the tapes and bring back those with potentially relevant data. Legacy backup tapes frequently hold substantial amounts of data, and they can be costly and time-consuming to restore. However, if tapes are managed appropriately and smartly, targeted tape restoration can be less painful than it sounds, should it become necessary.

Depending on the circumstances of a collection, you can use backup tapes as a source of electronically stored information (ESI). In some cases, collecting substantial amounts of network data from the live server can negatively impact system performance so that a backup tape may be a better alternative.

In other circumstances, restoring data for the last tape backup or a tape proximate to the relevant period may prove more efficient or appropriate. In some cases, creating a custom backup tape as a method of preservation should future processing becomes necessary may be the best answer. You should thoroughly analyze the utility of using tapes for collection if they are not the only location to collect relevant ESI.

Will changing the network infrastructure in favor of smartphone access make data networks more reliable or stable? That depends on the safeguards and technologies put in place. A corporate network is more than just people. The human beings behind those machines should be treated with respect. Lines of authority, where they exist, should be recognized. And those new to the company or the industry should be assisted where possible.

A corporation that is united has advantages over companies that allow individual tech-gurus to do their own thing without regard to others. Those who demonstrate technical professionalism can carve out a niche for themselves in support of changing corporate networks.

INFORMATION GATHERING

Information Gathering describes the process of acquiring knowledge by investigating, analyzing, and studying everything related to your target. The foundation for any successful penetration test is solid reconnaissance. Failure to perform proper information gathering will have you flailing around at random, attacking machines that are not vulnerable, and missing others that are. In this chapter, we cover just five of the many available information gathering techniques.

1. Preparing Metasploit for Port Scanning

Scanners and most other auxiliary modules use the RHOSTS option instead of RHOST. RHOSTS can take IP ranges, CIDR ranges, multiple ranges separated by commas, and line-separated host list files. By default, all of the scanner modules have the 'THREADS' value set to '1'. The 'THREADS' value sets the number of concurrent threads to use while scanning. Set this value to a higher number to speed up your scans or keep it lower to reduce network traffic but be sure to adhere to the following guidelines:

Keep the THREADS value under 16 on native Win32 systems
Keep THREADS under 200 when running MSF under Cygwin
On Unix-like operating systems, THREADS can be set as high as 256.

- Nmap & db_nmap

You can use the db_nmap command to run Nmap, the Network Mapper, which is a free security scanner against your targets, and your scan results would then be stored automatically in your database. However, if you also wish to import the scan results into another application or framework, later on, you will likely want to export the scan results in XML format. It is always nice to have all three Nmap outputs (xml, grepable, and normal). So you can run the Nmap scan using the *-oA* flag followed by the desired filename to generate the three output files, then issue the *db_import* command to populate the Metasploit database.

Run Nmap with the options you would normally use from the command line. If you wish for your scan to be saved to your database, you would omit the output flag and use *db_nmap*.

In addition to running Nmap, there are a variety of other port scanners that are available to us within the framework. For the sake of comparison, you can compare your Nmap scan results for port 80 with a Metasploit scanning module. First, let's determine what hosts had port 80 open, according to Nmap.

The Nmap scan you ran earlier was a SYN scan, so you run the same scan across the subnet looking for port 80 through our eth0 interface, using Metasploit. Now you can load up the 'tcp' scanner and use it against another target. This scanner uses the 'RHOSTS' option. You can issue the *hosts -R* command to automatically set this option with the hosts found in your database.

You can see that Metasploit's built-in scanner modules are more than capable of finding systems and open ports for you. It's just another excellent tool to have in your arsenal if you happen to be running Metasploit on a system without Nmap installed.

- SMB Version Scannin
:

Now that you have determined which hosts are available on the network, you can attempt to determine the operating systems they are running. This action helps you narrow down your attacks to target a specific system and stops you from wasting time on those that aren't vulnerable to a particular exploit.

Since there are many systems in your scan that have port 445 open, you will use the *scanner/smb/version* module to determine which version of Windows is running on a target and which Samba version (Samba is the standard Windows interoperability suite of programs for Linux and Unix) is on a Linux host.

Also, notice that if you issue the *hosts* command now, the newly-acquired information is stored in Metasploit's database.

- Idle Scanning

Nmap's IPID Idle scanning allows ethical hackers to be a little stealthy, scanning a target while spoofing the IP address of another host on the network. For this type of scan to work, you need to locate a host that is idle on the network and uses IPID sequences of either Incremental or Broken Little-Endian

Incremental. Metasploit contains the module *scanner/ip/ipidseq* to scan and look for a host that fits the requirements. In the free online Nmap book [https://nmap.org/book/man-book.html], you can find out more information on Nmap Idle Scanning.

Judging by the results of your scan, you have several potential zombies you can use to perform idle scanning. Now try scanning a host using the zombie, for example, at 192.168.1.109 and see if you get the same results you had earlier.

2. Using Metasploit to Find Vulnerable MSSQL Systems

Searching for and locating *MSSQL* (Microsoft SQL Server) installations inside the internal network can be achieved using UDP foot-printing. When MSSQL installs, it installs either on TCP port 1433 or a randomized dynamic TCP port. If the port is dynamically attributed, querying UDP port 1434 will provide you with information on the server, including the TCP port on which the service is listening.

Start searching for and load the MSSQL *ping* module inside the msfconsole. The first command you need to issue is to search for any mssql plugins. The second set of instructions is the *use scanner/mssql/mssql_ping*, and this loads the scanner module for you. Next, the command *show options* allows us to see what we need to specify. The *set RHOSTS 10.211.55.1/24* sets the subnet range you want to start looking for SQL servers on. You could specify a /16 or whatever you want to go after. The author recommends increasing the number of threads as this could take a long time with a single-threaded scanner. After the *run* command is issued, a scan is going to be performed and pull back specific information about the MSSQL server.

At this point, you could use the scanner/mssql/mssql_login module to brute-force the password by passing the module a dictionary file. Alternatively, you could also use medusa, or THC-Hydra - a parallelized login cracker which supports numerous protocols to attack - to do this. Once you successfully guess the password, there is a module for executing the *xp_cmdshell* stored procedure. Looking at the output of the *net user bacon ihazpassword /ADD*, you have successfully added a user account named "bacon", from there we could issue *net localgroup administrators bacon /ADD* to get a local administrator on the system itself.

Congratulations, you have now gained full control over the system at this point!

3. Scanning Services Using Metasploit

Again, other than using Nmap to perform scanning for services on your target network, Metasploit also includes a large variety of scanners for various services, often helping you determine potentially vulnerable running services on target machines.

- SSH Service

Let's assume a previous scan shows you have TCP port 22 open on two machines. SSH is very secure, but vulnerabilities are not unheard of, and it always pays to gather as much information as possible from your targets. You need to load up the *ssh_version* auxiliary scanner and issue the *set* command to set the 'RHOSTS' option. From there, you can run the module by merely typing *run*.

- FTP Service

Poorly configured FTP servers can frequently be the foothold you need to gain access to an entire network, so it always pays off to check to see if anonymous access is allowed whenever you encounter an open FTP port, which is usually on TCP port 21.

Please set the 'THREADS' to '1' here as you are only going to scan 1 host. In a short amount of time and with very little work, you can acquire a great deal of information about the hosts residing on your network, thus providing you with a much better picture of what you are facing when conducting your penetration test.

There are too many scanners available on the to showcase in this book. It is clear; however, the Metasploit Framework is well suited for all your scanning and identification needs.

4. Password Sniffing with Metasploit

Max Moser, a specialist in Computer Security and passionate hacker, released a Metasploit password sniffing module named *psnuffle* that sniffs passwords off the wire similar to the tool *dsniff*. It currently supports POP3, IMAP, FTP, and HTTP GET.

Using the *psnuffle* module is extremely simple. There are some options available, but the module works great "out of the box." There are some options available, including the ability to import a *pcap* capture file. You can run the *psnuffle* scanner in its default mode to capture a successful FTP login. It is an excellent tool for passive information gathering.

5. SNMP Auxiliary Module for Metasploit

Continuing with your information gathering, let's take a look at *SNMP Sweeping*. SNMP sweeps are often good at finding a ton of information about a specific system or compromising the remote device. If you can find a Cisco device running a private string, for example, you can download the entire device configuration, modify it, and upload your malicious configuration. Often the passwords themselves are level 7 encoded, which means they are trivial to decode and obtain the *enable* or login password for the specific device.

Metasploit comes with a built-in auxiliary module specifically for sweeping SNMP devices. There are a couple of things to understand before we perform our SNMP scan. First, '*read only*' and '*read write*' community strings play an important role in what type of information can be extracted or modified on the devices themselves. If you can "guess" the *read-only* or *read-write* strings, you can obtain quite a bit of access you wouldn't typically have. Besides, if Windows-based devices are configured with SNMP, often with the RO/RW community strings, you can extract patch levels, services running, last reboot times, usernames on the system, routes, and various other amounts of information that are valuable to an attacker.

By default, Metasploitable's SNMP service only listens on the localhost. Many of the examples demonstrated here require you to change these default settings. Open and edit /etc/default/snmpd, and change the following from:
SNMPDOPTS='-Lsd -Lf /dev/null -u snmp -I -smux -p /var/run/snmp.pid
to:
SNMPDOPTS='-Lsd -Lf /dev/null -u snmp -I -smux -p /var/run/snmp.pid 0.0.0.0'

A service restart is needed for the changes to take effect. Once restarted, you will now be able to scan the service from your attacking machine.

- SNMP Enum

We can gather lots of information when using SNMP scanning modules such as open ports, services, hostname, processes, and uptime, to name a few. Using your Metasploitable virtual machine as your target, you can run the *auxiliary/scanner /snmp/snmp_enum* module and see what information it provides you. First, you load the module and set the 'RHOST' option using the information stored in your workspace. Using *hosts* -R sets this option for you.

- Reviewing your SNMP Scan

The output of your SNMP scan provides you with a wealth of information on your target system. You can see lots of relevant information about your target, such as its processor type, or process IDs.

NETWORK SCANNING

Scanning is a set of procedures for identifying live hosts, ports, and services, discovering operating systems and architecture of target systems, identifying vulnerabilities and threats within a network. Network scanning is one of the components of intelligence gathering and information retrieving mechanism a hacker can use to create an overview scenario and a profile of the target organization. This goal is achieved by using sophisticated and aggressive reconnaissance techniques.

There are three different types of scanning processes, namely, Network Scanning, Port Scanning, and Vulnerability Scanning.
  I. Network Scanning delivers information such as live host computers, IP addresses, operating systems, system architecture, topology details, installed firewalls, and trusted routers information.
  II. Port Scanning helps to detect open ports and services running on the target network.
  III. Vulnerability scanning leads hackers to identify weak spots, such as missing patches, unnecessary services, weak authentication, or weak encryption algorithm.

  I.   Network Scanning

Network Security consists of a set of rules, policies, and instructions that are accepted to monitor and prevent the misuse and unauthorized manipulation of a network.
Network scanning deals with Network Security, and this is an activity that identifies network vulnerabilities and the loopholes to safeguard your network from unwanted and unusual behavior that can harm your system, or even your personal and confidential information.
Network Scanning is a process that can be defined in many ways, and it identifies the active hosts (Clients and Servers) on a network and their activities to attack a network. It is also being used by attackers to hack the system. This procedure is used for system maintenance and security assessment of a network.

The best recommended Network Scanning Tools are:
- *Acunetix Online* includes a fully automated network scanning tool that detects and reports on over 50,000 known network vulnerabilities and misconfigurations.
- *OpenVAS (Vulnerability Assessment System)* is a free network security scanning tool. Its primary component is the Security Scanner, which runs in the Linux environment only. It can be integrated with Open Vulnerability Assessment Language (OVAL) to write vulnerability tests.
- *Angry IP Scanner* is a free and open-source network scanning utility with the ability to scan IP addresses and also performs port scan effectively and rapidly.
- *Advanced IP Scanner* is a free and open-source network scanning tool that works in the Windows environment. It can detect and scan any device on a network including, wireless devices.
- *Qualys Freescan* is a free and open-source network scanning tool that provides scans for URLs, Internet IPs, and local servers to detect security loopholes.
- *SoftPerfect Network Scanner* is a freeware network scanning utility with advanced scanning features known as Multi-thread IPv4/IPv6 Scanning.
- *Retina Network Security Scanner* is a vulnerability scanner and solution that also provides security patches for Microsoft, Adobe, and Firefox applications.
- *Nmap* maps your network and its ports numerically; hence, it is also known as Port Scanning Tool. Nmap comes with NSE (Nmap Scripting Engine) scripts to detect network security issues and misconfiguration.
- *Nessus* is a widely used network security scanner that works with the UNIX system.

II.   Port Scanning

Port Scanning is the name for the technique used to identify open ports and services available on a network host. It is sometimes utilized by security technicians to audit computers for vulnerabilities; however, it is also used by hackers to target victims. It can be used to send requests to connect to the targeted computers, and then keep track of the ports which appear to be open, or those that respond to the request.

Hackers typically utilize port scanning because it is an easy way in which they can quickly discover services they can break into. In some cases, hackers can even open the ports themselves to access the targeted computer. Hackers also use port scanners to conduct tests for open ports on Personal Computers that are connected to the web. Port scanners are some of the most useful tools when you are starting your security investigation on any remote or local network.

Used by programmers, system and network administrators, Port Scanning Tools are applications designed to scan servers and hosts to check what available ports are being used for network communications. Once the scan has finished, you can run other security penetration and exploit tests to verify how strong the current security policies are.

The top 5 best Port Scanners currently available are:
- *Nmap* stands for Network mapper, and it is a free and open-source application used by system administrators, developers and network engineers for security auditing on local and remote networks. Available for Linux, Windows and Mac OS, it can be run from the classic command-line terminal, or by using a GUI interface. Also used for Network Scanning.
- *Unicornscan* is widely known because of its asynchronous TCP and UDP scanning capabilities, along with non-common network discovery patterns that provide alternative ways to explore details about remote operating systems and services.
- *Angry IP Scanner* (see description above as a Network Scanner)
- *Netcat* can be used for an extensive range of objectives, like open remote connections, tunneling and proxying, run remote commands, as well as port scanning.
- *Zenmap is the official Nmap Front End interface (GUI)*. For those who are not familiar with command line terminals, *Nmap* creators launched this GUI release that allows you to scan remote hosts in a fancy and friendly way.

III.   Vulnerability Assessment Scanning or Vulnerability Analysis.

The method of recognizing, categorizing, and characterizing the security holes among the network infrastructure, computers, hardware system, and software is known as Vulnerability Analysis. A few examples of such vulnerabilities are like a misconfiguration of components in network infrastructure, a defect or error in an operating system, or any ambiguity in a marketable product. If vulnerabilities are found as a part of any vulnerability assessment, then there is a need for vulnerability disclosure. Generally, such disclosures are carried out by separate teams like Computer Emergency Readiness Team (CERT) or the organization which has discovered the vulnerability.

The vulnerabilities mentioned above become the leading source for malicious activities like cracking the systems, LANs, and websites. To evaluate or assess the security of any network, an ethical hacker needs to focus activities on the following six steps:
1) Spot and realize the approach of your industry or company like how it is structured and managed.
2) Trace the systems, data, and applications that are exercised throughout the practice of the business.
3) Investigate the unseen data sources which can permit simple entry to the protected information.
4) Classify both the physical and virtual servers that run the necessary business applications.
5) Tracking all the existing security measures which are already implemented.
6) Inspect the network for any vulnerability.

There are several Vulnerability Scanner Tools available on the market, here is a selection of the best:
- *Netsparker* is a highly accurate automated scanner that identifies vulnerabilities such as SQL Injection and Cross-site Scripting in web applications and web APIs.
- *Acunetix* is a fully automated web vulnerability scanner that detects and reports on over 4500 web application vulnerabilities, including all variants of SQL Injection and XSS.
- *Intruder* is a proactive vulnerability scanner that scans you as soon as new vulnerabilities are released. Besides, it has over 10,000 historic security checks, including for WannaCry, Heartbleed, and SQL Injection.
- *Probely* scans your Web Applications to find vulnerabilities or security issues and guides on how to fix them, having developers in mind.
- *ManageEngine Vulnerability Manager Plus* is an on-premise threat and vulnerability management solution that empowers IT administrators and security teams with an integrated console to secure systems and servers across local and remote offices, roaming devices as well as closed network (DMZ) machines.
- *OpenVAS* serves as a convenient service that provides tools for both vulnerability scanning and vulnerability management.

- *Nikto* is an open-source web scanner used to assess probable issues and vulnerabilities.
- *Wireshark* is the world's leading and extensively used network protocol analyzer.
- *Aircrack* is also called as *Aircrack-NG*, which is a set of tools used to assess the WiFi network security.
- *Nessus Professional* is a patented and branded vulnerability scanner developed by Tenable Network Security.
- *Retina CS Community* is an open-source and web-based console with which the vulnerability management has been centralized and simplified.
- *Microsoft Baseline Security Analyzer* is a free Microsoft tool used to secure a Windows computer based on the guidelines or specifications set by Microsoft.
- *Secunia Personal Software Inspector* is a free program used to find the security vulnerabilities on your PC and even solving them fast.

BANNER GRABBING

A server banner is a particular greeting message sent by a server running on a host. It is imperative to hide this information as it may contain essential strings that can help hackers to find breaks on a system. Banner grabbing is a technique used to gain information about a computer system on a network and the services running on its open ports. Administrators can use this to take inventory of the systems and services on their network.

However, an intruder can use banner grabbing to find network hosts that are running versions of applications and operating systems with known exploits. Banner grabbing can also be defined as connecting to remote applications and observing the output. This activity can be surprisingly informative to remote attackers.

Similarly, corporate network/system administrators can exploit this ability to detect how vulnerable their networks are. At the very least, one may have identified the make and model of the running services, which in many cases, is enough to set the vulnerability research process in motion. Some examples of service ports used for banner grabbing are those used by HyperText Transfer Protocol (HTTP), File Transfer Protocol (FTP), and Simple Mail Transfer Protocol (SMTP); ports 80, 21, and 25 respectively.

As already mentioned, a banner grabber is nothing but a tool that can be used to extract information from application banners. Ethical hackers can also use it during penetration tests. Malicious hackers use banner grabbing since the technique can reveal compromising information about the services that are running on a system. The technique works by using banner grabbing tools and a proprietary program to establish a connection with a remote machine, after which a bad request is sent. That causes a vulnerable host to respond with a banner message, which may contain information that malicious hackers can use to compromise the system further.

Tools commonly used to perform banner grabbing are *Telnet*, *Nmap*, and *Netcat*. For example, one could establish a connection to a target web server using such a tool, then send an HTTP request. The response typically contains information about the service running on the host.

- Banner Grabbing Using *Netcat*

Netcat is a networking utility that reads and writes data across network connections, using the TCP/IP protocol. It is designed to be a reliable "back-end" tool that can be used directly or easily driven by other programs and scripts. At the same time, it is a feature-rich network debugging and exploration tool, since it can create almost any kind of connection you would need and has several impressive built-in capabilities. *Netcat* provides access to the following main features:

Outbound or inbound connections, TCP or UDP, to or from any ports
Full DNS forward/reverse checking, with appropriate warnings
Ability to use any local source port
Ability to use any locally-configured network source address
Built-in port-scanning capabilities, with randomizer
Built-in loose source-routing capability
Can read command line arguments from standard input
Optional ability to let another program service inbound connection

- Banner Grabbing Using *Telnet*

You can telnet to hosts on the default telnet port (TCP port 23) to see whether you are presented with a login prompt or any other information. Just enter the following line at the command prompt in Windows or UNIX:
telnet ip_address
You can telnet to other commonly used ports with these commands:
SMTP: telnet ip_address 25
HTTP: telnet ip_address 80
POP3: telnet ip_address 110

- Countermeasures against Banner Grabbing attacks

The following steps can reduce the chance of banner grabbing attacks:
If there isn't a business need for services that offer banner information, disable those unused services on the network host.
If there isn't a business need for the default banners, or if you can customize the banners, configure the network host's application or operating system to either disable the banners or remove information from the banners that could give an attacker a leg up.

ENUMERATION

Enumeration is defined as the process of extracting user names, machine names, network resources, shares, and services from a system. The gathered information is used to identify the vulnerabilities or weak points in system security and tries to exploit the system gaining phase.

Enumeration consists in exploiting the characteristics of a particular service to obtain as much information as possible. This action is a process where the attacker establishes an active connection with the victim and tries to discover as many attack vectors as possible, which can be used to exploit the systems further.

User enumeration is when a malicious actor can use brute-force to either guess or confirm valid users in a system. User enumeration is often a web application vulnerability, though it can also be found in any system that requires user authentication.

Enumeration can be used to gain information on:
Network resources and shares
SNMP data and DNS details
IP and routing tables
Usernames and groups of different systems
Passwords policies lists
Auditing and service setting
Machine names
Applications and banners

Enumeration depends on the services that the systems offer, such as:
DNS enumeration
NTP enumeration
SNMP enumeration
Linux/Windows enumeration
SMB enumeration

Tools that are widely used for Enumeration are:

- *NTP Suite* is used for NTP enumeration. It is important because, in a network environment, you can find other primary servers that help the hosts to update their times, and you can do it without authenticating the system.
- *enum4linux* is used to enumerate Linux systems. smtp-user-enum
- *smtp-user-enum* tries to guess usernames by using SMTP service.

CONCLUSION

The author hopes that this book provides the readers with a general understanding of ethical hacking, with essential knowledge for further self-learning, and enable a deep-dive into the vast topic of cybersecurity.

Your journey started when you first opened this book and ended with reaching this chapter. On the way, you faced a lot of information and knowledge to absorb, but don't let the aspiring hacker inside you be discouraged by such obstacles. If you manage to look at these hurdles as a personal challenge, then you will most likely be able to hack anything and penetrate even sophisticated systems.

Let's go briefly through the topics explained and the knowledge you gained by reading "Ethical Hacking: The Complete Beginners Guide to Basic Security and Penetration Testing." In this book, the author explains the basic concepts, importance, and the advantages of ethical hacking. The book further describes lab building methods for ethical hacking experiments, mind maps, network theory, company networks, and information collection concepts, as well as, provides examples, forms, and the uses of ethical hacking. Topics like exploitation and post-exploitation were left out on purpose but should be taken into consideration in advance stages of your hacking experience, and confidence.

You now possess all the necessary basics and the fundamental knowledge of ethical hacking. As you prepare to put your skills to the test, you can now consider yourself a *White Hat Ethical Hacker*.

ABOUT THE AUTHOR

Marc Stanford holds a Master's degree in Advanced Computer Science and currently works on his Doctoral Thesis on Neural Networks. During his professional career, he is specialized, among others, in artificial intelligence and complex data modeling.

Although already experienced in tutoring and lecturing, writing technical books is Marc's newest passion. He lives and works in Palo Alto, CA, USA.

Also, by Marc Stanford

Programming with Python
An Easy to Understand Beginners Guide to Coding with Python

Non-fiction, eBook and paperback published in October 2019, ISBN-13: 9781696419642, available at Amazon in all marketplaces